SACRED BUTTERFLIES:
POEMS, PRAYERS AND PRACTICES

by

Jim Conlon

Paying Attention to Other Modes of Understanding

SACRED BUTTERFLIES:
POEMS, PRAYERS AND PRACTICES:
Paying Attention to Other Modes of Understanding

by James Conlon

Library of Congress
LOC 2013942579
ISBN 978-1-55605-452-5

EBook Version 978-1-55605-453-2

Cover Photograph by Adriane Grimaldi, used by permission

Wyndham Hall Press
5050 Kerr Rd.
Lima, OH 45806

As I read *Sacred Butterflies*, I had the feeling of being empowered, for these practices have proven their worth, both for Conlon and the other spiritual leaders he draws upon. And there was a second, unexpected benefit: a surprising peace came just from knowing I was participating in processes that have supported such deep souls. If Jim Conlon's spiritual practices have worked for him and these of his teachers, there is every reason to believe they will work for us, as well.
— Brian Thomas Swimme
co-author (w/ Mary Evelyn Tucker) *The Journey of the Universe*

With the heart of a poet and deeply imbued by the spirit of Thomas Berry, Jim Conlon illuminates the wonder and beauty of this ever-changing world, lifting up creation as a sacrament of ineffable love. This is a beautiful book that can be used for prayer groups, faith formation, or private meditation. The reader will return many times to passages or words and ponder over and over again the marvelous work of our Creator God.
— Ilia Delio, OSF Georgetown University

A book of wisdom to nurture the heart, energize the mind, and sustain a hope-filled spirit.
— Joyce Rupp, author of *My Soul Feels Lean,* and *Praying Our Goodbyes*

Seldom can we enjoy such intelligence, vision, and inspiration in one fine place! Read Jim Conlon's offering of words and let them lead you far beyond words—into a big and beautiful world.
— Fr. Richard Rohr, OFM
Center for Action and Contemplation, Albuquerque, NM

Drawing on the gift of mythopoetic imagination—through prayer and poetry—Jim Conlon illuminates the subtle and empowering movements of the spirit in the experience of everyday life. A valuable resource for daily reflection.
— Diarmuid O'Murchu, Sacred Heart Missionary Order

Steeped in life's rich experience, Jim Conlon scatters a wealth of seeds to energize and empower us to seek geo-justice and geo-wisdom. I love the zest for life, sense of divine nearness, strength of engagement and vividness of feeling expressed in these haunting lines that can inspire our dreams, nourish our souls, and make us see the blessings present in the joys and pains of our daily lives. This book is alive with the heartbeat of hope—may it reach, awaken, and surprise all those in search of a dream and a vision to guide them.
— Ursula King
Institute of Advanced Studies, University of Bristol, England

Poetry, prayer, and practice: how tenderly Jim Conlon uses these forms to bring heaven to earth; to proclaim the presence of hope *in a withering world,* to celebrate truth beauty and goodness even as the wounded and weeping break open our hearts.
— Roger Housden, author of the *Ten Poems Series*

Jim Conlon's collected poems, prayers and spiritual practices are sacred butterflies—light and ephemeral like butterflies, yet each is a sacramental presence of the divine. These are vehicles of the spiritual journey that integrate the interior life and our struggle with the world around us. Sacred and secular are united, the universe itself recognized as a manifestation of the divine. Dip into this collection at any point and let the flow of creative transformation circulate in your own life. Jim Conlon has distilled the best of his years of reflection and hope in these pieces and offered them to us as a modest and precious gift.
— Rosemary Radford Ruether, PhD
Claremont School of Theology

TABLE OF CONTENTS

v

DEDICATION

I dedicate these pages to two great archetypal figures who have been significant in my life and the lives of many others.

To Thomas Merton (1915–1968), who wrote to the world from the Trappist monastery Gethsemane Abbey in the hills of Kentucky; in his prose, poetry and art (drawings and photographs), he provided the architecture of the spiritual journey and demonstrated his gifts as the Master of the Soul.

To Thomas Berry (1914–2009), cultural historian and geologian, whose visionary life began in the monastery of the Congregation of the Passion Community and extended to China, university teaching and the Center of Religious Research (where he composed his most important work), and whose writing has inspired a generation of seekers to celebrate the universe story and the great work, themes that dominate his most important work and earned him the name Master of the Cosmos.

ACKNOWLEDGMENTS

I celebrate and give thanks to my many companions whose inspiration and support have made this project possible.

I am indebted to my Holy Names University/Sophia Center students, colleagues and friends, who have contributed in many ways to the poems, prayers and practices included in these pages.

In particular, I want to express great thanks to the following for their presence in my life and contribution to this work: Niahm Brennan, Youngmin Song, Mary Whelan, Robert Lopez, Marilyn Goddard and Grace Larra.

I want to thank Jude Berman, whose editorial gifts guided the creation of the book, and Mark McCullough at Wyndham Hall Press for his support, which made possible the publishing of *Sacred Butterflies*.

PREFACE

Over the years, I have met and worked with many courageous souls who dedicate their lives to the empowerment of others and to the evocation of beauty across the planet. They give so much to make it possible for harmony, balance and peace to flow among all. Yet I have observed that many who do justice work sooner or later burn out because they have sacrificed their own spiritual nourishment on the mistaken assumption that self-nourishment and interiority will not serve others. As a result, they lose touch with the sense of joy that springs from working toward the upliftment of humanity and our planet, which put them on the path in the first place, and instead resort to glum plodding. At worst, they sink into apathy.

The spiritual journey calls out for a dynamic integration of the interior life with our experience of the world around us. To be a fully integrated person, you could say we are called to be both a poet and a politician.

Toward this end, I have prepared the material in *Sacred Butterflies*. Through poems, prayers and practices, we can stimulate the imagination and tap into the wisdom of the heart, and thus draw sustenance for our work in the world. I have found these three modes to be trusty companions on the journey, and wish to share them with you that you may benefit from them, as well.

This book is organized into three distinct sections: Let the Cosmos Speak (poems), Paying Attention to Each Sacred Moment (prayer) and Cultivating Habits of the Heart (spiritual practice). However, you will find overlap between them. For example, you can compose a prayer in the form of a poem. Or you can write a poem about the power of prayer. Similarly, the spiritual practices you choose can involve prayer or the writing of poetry.

1

I have shared poems and prayers that emerged from my own creative process and the practices that have been of value to me. Please enjoy them, but don't stop there. *Sacred Butterflies* is meant not only be read in a passive manner but to serve as an inspiration and invitation to give voice to what lies deep within.

As an individual, you can reflect on these poems, prayers and practices and select those that resonate with you. May the words and ideas flow into your depths and moisten your heart and soul. As you respond in your own way, I invite you to let go of outcomes, to allow surprises to upset your plans. Like a river that visits all the crevices and rivulets along its banks, let your journey flow where it will. Venture forth and embrace the unknown as your path ahead reveals itself and the going becomes ever clearer.

You can also use *Sacred Butterflies* in a classroom or group setting. At Sophia Center, we hold classes and workshops in which participants write poems or prayers and share them, as we support one another to go out and engage with the world.

INTRODUCTION

We live today enveloped in a defining moment, an epicenter of hope, possibility and challenge. Can you perceive it? With a felt sense of an irreversible emergence, we move forward together, guided by the undulating waves of the new story. With a new set of eyes, like theater goers in a 3D movie, we see bubbling up in our midst the contours of a more mutually enhancing world, longed for but not yet realized.

From Descartes to de Chardin, Bacon to Berry, Newton to Swimme, prophetic voices have generously dispensed their sacraments of hope and revitalized our journey.

Buoyed by a new mythopoetic imagination, we are invited to tell a story, compose a poem, pay attention to our prayers and articulate our practices. A language arises from the floorboard of our souls that can coalesce into a gospel for the way ahead.

Now is the time to embrace the mystery, gaze longingly in awe and wonder at the stars, and respond to the aspirations of the heart. Ponder your place in the great work, fulfill your destiny, unleash your passion and purpose, and become convinced that tomorrow will be more beautiful than all the preceding pasts.

Called forth by the unique needs and possibilities of this defining moment in human/Earth history, we descend into the recesses of our soul. We discover in the depths of our psyche that there are as many galaxies within as there are without. From this poetic place that lies beyond conscious thought, we take up the challenge to build a scaffolding of praxis and hope.

As we awaken to a new vision and place for our great work, we feel immersed in and moved by this moment of grace that propels us to take our place in the transformation of the world.

Honor your legacy and common roots. We all came from the fireball, we all came from Africa. Today we emerge from the stirring in the culture and discover there a rich diversity of race, background and preference. With the lyrics of the Baptist hymn we joyfully say:

Red, yellow, black or white
We are all precious in God's sight.

Sometimes uncertainty surrounds us. There seems to be no purpose or value to what at one time we thought was perhaps our gift. This is not the time to rest, but to keep going. These moments can be an incubation period, a time when something previously unexpressed is asking to be born.

As we venture forth into uncharted territory, guided by an emerging story, we search for guidance and grounding in our journey. To manifest what lies deep within, let the cosmos speak (poems), pay attention to each new revelatory moment (prayer) and engage fully in the sacredness of existence through participation in patterns of living that will empower an enduring quest to achieve fully the identity and purpose for which we were created (practice).

Each year, hundreds of thousands of monarch butterflies migrate vast distances to winter in various spots in California. Though they are a new generation of butterflies, they return to the same trees where butterflies have wintered over the years, gathering as if companions on the way. As we enter a new defining moment in human/Earth history, let us take a lesson from these creatures: that we, in fact, belong to each other as we take up with even greater vigor our call to the great work.

At what Lawren Harris called the "summit of our soul," we celebrate through poems, prayers and practices as we imagine new avenues of intimacy and mystery. From life's inevitable caterpillar phase of prolonged engagement, through the transformational chrysalis stage, we find fulfillment and arrive at our sacred butterfly destiny, and throughout we are joined by good companions on the way. May the pages that follow accompany you on your journey so you blossom forth and become the sacred butterfly you are called to be.

Perhaps puzzled by uncertainty and waiting for what is being asked of us at this moment, we respond to the wisdom of Thomas Berry, who advised us that when the path ahead appears unclear, the best thing we can do is to write a poem. What Thomas meant was, when the path before us seems clouded and unclear, we can search for guidance and direction by gaining access to another mode of understanding.

To write a poem is to allow our soul to speak, to sink into our psyche and let the words arise, unfiltered by analysis or abstraction. From this place, we gain access to what is imaginative, intuitive and a source of deeper wisdom than the mind can discern, express or understand.

Another vehicle into the unknown future is what often is referred to as prayer. By prayer I do not mean a reversion to inordinate self-consciousness. I also do not mean a pious plea for guidance and direction. Rather, I mean an enhanced awareness of the ocean of sacredness that life offers, a greater capacity to notice the ebb and flow of existence.

Finally, practice allows us to attune our actions to the dynamics of life's unfolding and empowers us to live in alignment with our prayers and the highest intentions expressed through our poems and stories.

Through poem, prayer and practice, we strive to create balance and direction in the up-start spring of existence as we plan and discover the next steps on this journey.

Through poem, prayer and practice we activate and illumine all for which we long, anticipate and hope. Perhaps through these processes and practices we will keep alive within and around us a vision realized daily in acts of compassion and gestures of generosity. We look forward with increased confidence to the day when our dreams will be realized and our struggles transformed.

SECTION I:

LET THE COSMOS SPEAK: POEMS

Poems

When I think of poetry, I recall the line from a poem I heard in grade school: "Tiger, tiger burning bright"—words by William Blake that I committed to memory and that remain with me today. I have been inspired by many poets whose words pierce my heart and tug at my soul, among them Rainer Maria Rilke, John O'Donohue and Mary Oliver. I often reflect on Thomas Berry's suggestion that perhaps the best thing we can do is to write a poem. He says poetry takes us to a new place of understanding. I have found that this is true for me.

Poetry has been a vehicle for me to reach what lies deep within and to express it without becoming entangled in too much rational thought. The psyche is able to transcend the abstract left brain while capturing the great gift of human language that originates in the imagistic, holistic right brain.

I sit in my apartment in Berkeley, California, pick up a pen and a pad of paper, and begin to write. For a period of time, inspired after I attended a reading by Mary Oliver, I took up the challenge each day to listen deeply to the spirit speaking softly to my soul and commit that to paper.

Poetry affords the opportunity to have a dialogue with the pad of paper. The paper serves as a dialogical partner, a spiritual companion, whose empty page is the willing recipient of whatever lies in my heart and longs to be heard.

Sometimes I think of poetry as a dream on paper—a way to translate the impulses of the soul into shareable forms.

Poetry gives expression to blessings, to intuitive images that hover in the human psyche, beyond the embrace of ordinary conscious thought. Poetry is the midwife of those sacred impulses that emerge from another world, the land of the preconscious.

Poetry is prayer. Words arise from the inmost self and emerge unbidden from it, as an incense of hope and inspiration for the invisible incarnate one.

Poetry is a heart language that can give expression to the cosmos, where hidden hopes and aspirations lie.

Poems are the manifestations of a marinated soul. They offer a birth canal where unborn articulations of life's great mysteries emerge into the conscious world to reveal past journeys and predict future paths.

The poem is an oracle, a golden thread that makes visible for a passing moment a road map of our destiny through another mode of understanding.

There is so much to ponder, and so many doorways of surprise. Touch the mystery, bow in humble admiration to the words that come from another place and find expression on the landscape of Earth.

All is welcome now, everyone is present: the turtle and the polliwog, the poem and the person. Each is a lyric of life, a declaration of inspiration and hope.

Poetry is the art form of the mystic, the clarion call of the prophet.

Poetic words originate from another place; they tell of truths and narratives not yet understood.

Poems are canaries; they tell of safety and peril.

Poems are songs of yesterday and tomorrow announced today.

Poems pay attention to what our world has overlooked; they speak of other worlds and take us to a new time and space and understanding.

Poems announce the morning and bid farewell to night. They discover divinity in surprising places—in books, cornfields, sleepless nights, sunshine and sorrow, and in creatures great and small.

When I write a poem, I gain insight into my personal life and the pathology and promise of the world around me. I feel the pain of death, so prevalent in my midst: death in the streets; death to the visions of youth and dreams of old; death in my heart; yes, even the possible death of Earth.

Yet in the midst of it all, I experience hope, and wonder why. Is there not hope in the hearts of many when a child is born?

There is hope when a flower bursts forth from a crack in a broken sidewalk. There is hope when night turns to day, winter to spring. And in the immeasurable moment we know from our tradition, death turns into life; we call this "resurrection."

Poems tell courageous tales of love and loss and hopes not yet realized.

Poems are proclamations of amazement. They are always accompanied by beyondness, yet fully immersed in the mud and waters of life.

Live Just for Today

Let every impulse rise
like daisies in the field—
impulses in the soul;
in a withering world, hope.

This, dear ones, we are called to do:
to sit by the fire of Earth's aspiration
till what we long for
begins to emerge.

Friends of all who swim, run, fly,
join tomorrow's chorus.
Hope and prayer give courage
to live just for today.

Pen of Hope

Hope has put a pen in my hand.
Words hover in my soul and want to speak,
unknown, unheard, as yet unexpressed.

They want to speak of longing, mystery and love,
of the beauty that dresses the garden
with flowers, pink and blue.
They invite my tears to flow to heal the parched land,
quench the thirst that resides in every arid one.

Yes, hope has put a pen in my hand
to heal and wash away the pain of broken hearts,
of terror in the depths of each neglected one.

Invitation

Fireflies
exploding in the far-off sky
send forth
supernova,
cascading,
join their new companions,
whose showers of de-light
illuminate the night,
reveal a hidden path
to invite us home.

Notes of Wonder

Paying attention,
see with new eyes
the texture of the clouds,
hear with new ears
the song of a morning dove,
feel with new awareness
the gentleness of the rain,
smell the aroma
of the rose.

Every sight and sound,
every taste and smell,
becomes a note of beauty
in the symphony
of life.

Incarnation

This newborn robin
hungers for food.
In this moment,
open to the light of
sacred mystery.

Apertures of Hope

Doors open and close,
sleepy puppy opens one eye
to greet the day.

A day of threshold moments
where opportunities abound
to love, to hate, dream, wonder and come home.

Open your heart,
I hear the cosmos cry,
to beauty, wonder, violence
and great anticipation of all that
up to now remains undone.

Wake up! Like the puppy
greet the day,
engage in what's unfinished.

Welcome every new day,
bask in the sun,
embrace your planetary home.

Vitality, Decline and a Hopeful Heart

O the vitality of youth,
fearless, bullet proof and vain.

What about the stealth of declining years?

One less step,
vision fades, decibels decline.

The future now emerges
in a rearview mirror.

Yet in these moments
you cast upon the yesterdays a grateful eye.

In silence, thank the generous one
for all you have received

And welcome each new tomorrow
with a hopeful heart.

Wisdom and Wonder in It All

A lawyer in his retirement years collapses in a friend's arms.
A child wanders the streets at night,
searching bar to bar for her parent.
Flowers and mementos adorn a lamppost down the block,
a living memory for the victim of a drive-by shooting.

The media flood humanity, wash across our lives.

Yet beyond all the pain and devastation, goodness remains.
Flowers bloom, children play,
rivers flower and elders enjoy life.
Enduring hope lives in every beating heart,
and the deep conviction that there is meaning in it all.

The God of the cosmos,
God of love and life,
holds us in divine embrace,
gives meaning to our pain,
nourishes us with joy, gratitude and beauty.

Isn't this what Jesus came to teach?
To love beyond measure,
to forgive the instrument of pain,
to embrace peace and joy
and find wisdom and wonder in it all.

That All May Live

Now you know
that things are bad and beautiful,
that devastation happens
on a blue green planet.

Children are born,
health is challenged,
food is toxic, water unclean,
beauty deprived.

So, now that you know,
ponder the question:
What am I called to do?

Purify the poison,
heal the alienation,
embrace each other on the journey,
fulfill your own purpose,
that all may live.
Yes, that all may live.

The Shimmering Well

More than a collection of lumber and stone,
more than a place to live,
more than a hearth and symbol of home
is the Shimmering Well by the sea.

More than a beautiful building now in place,
more than a dream now come true,
more than a context to gather and talk
is the Shimmering Well by the sea.

More than a beautiful home for the restless heart,
more than a project for peace,
more than a haven to heal the soul
is the Shimmering Well by the sea.

More than a place to be equal and just,
more than a place to be free,
more than a place for the integral life
is the Shimmering Well by the sea.

More than a place to listen and learn,
more than a place to just be,
more than a place for beauty and balance
is the Shimmering Well by the sea.

Yes it's a place for stories and dreams,
a place of mystery for me,
as we build souls of justice and peace
at the Shimmering Well by the sea.

I met Mary Whelan in 1992, when she was a student at the Institute in Culture and Creation Spirituality (ICCS). Mary was the cofounder of a project in Dublin, Ireland, called the Community Action Network (CAN); she also co-authored a book about the project. For many years, Mary and her colleagues were involved in community development work in inner city Dublin; they worked with women who had endured domestic violence and with others confronted by substance abuse and various social needs.

When Mary arrived at ICCS, she began to look back at the work of her colleagues and she saw something had been lacking. She felt she could now contribute something she called "soul work." She understood this to be a spiritual energy and zest for life that would sustain and support her colleagues in their challenging work of community development.

With this vision, Mary set out to create a center on the shores of County Mayo. Later, I visited her at this site, which she named Turlain (the English translation of which is "Shimmering Well by the Sea"). Inspired by Mary's vision and supported by her years of good work, I composed this poem, which now hangs in a privileged place, honoring the soul work Mary envisioned during her days at ICCS.

A Declaration

There's a glimmer in the window,
Earth wakes up,
greets the day.

Everywhere new light
washes across creation.

Squirrel shouts, "Good morning,"
love proclaims the angelus,
a new day is born.

Each creature
a member of the choir
proclaiming songs of praise.

Resurrection

Birds sing,
breezes blow,
Sun announces the day.
New life springs forth
with a symphony of Easter.
The sweat lodge door lies open
to recall the empty tomb,
and resurrection rises once again.

Epic of Engagement

From the fireball of our own existence,
we discover within the opaqueness of pain and possibility,
a newfound ability to act
and heal a brokenhearted world.

We entertain and envision a home for the children
and are enveloped in a deep desire
to quench our thirst
for oneness with creation and our God.

With newfound appreciation for beauty
we resacralize the world
and discover in each expression of creation
fresh energy to understand the language of Earth.

With cosmic literacy and realization
we enter the promised land of home
and leave behind this time of pathos and pathology
to embark upon a flourishing landscape of hope.

Breaking free of structures of conformity
and enveloped in a divine embrace,
we wander forth into a land of new beginnings
and see in each a contribution to the reign of God.

We fashion forth
motifs of transformation
and learn again the language of the soul
to make audible the chorus of creation
as every voice is heard.

We traverse the doorway of engagement
and enact a paschal mystery story for our time,
listen to the great symphony of life,
dance amidst the sunshine and clouds,
make an act of evocation,
give praise to a great tsunami of hope.

In the stillness,
Earth speaks,
celebrate the wonder of it all.

Canticle of the Divine

I will rise, I will rise,
in the life of the people
I will rise.

In the lives of the people of this land,
I will rise, I will rise.

With the resurgence of Earth,
we will rise, we will rise.

With the spirit of the Divine,
we will rise, we will rise.

In the places of poverty,
in El Salvador's people,
in the heart of Guatemala,
there beats deep despair.

Beautiful lands, gardens of Eden,
are nations of martyrs
whose people are taking
the road to Golgotha.

The rich have been taking
the fruits of their labor,
the work of their hands.

Never again, Guatemala!
Your bishop's decree,
the decree of the crucified
people and planet.
Come down from the cross
of the army's oppression,
the cross of injustice,
the cross of despair.

Of violent homes,
of enduring illness,
of wages too meager,
of forest turned wasteland,
come down from the cross.

Let there be no more martyrs.
Let us rise, let us rise.
Sing a song of resurgence.

Welcome this Easter:
economic justice,
planetary peace,
rights for all creatures,
wholeness of land,
of all God's creation.

Let there be a New Easter,
fresh hope, celebration,
when Bishop Gerardi's
Guatemala: Never Again
is sung as a hymn of joy,
of longing, of liberation
everywhere, everywhere.

What is Justice?

What is justice?
Is it not the Great Work
of creating the conditions
by which beauty can shine forth?

What is justice?
Is it not dissolving dualism,
nurturing the conditions
that make mutuality possible?

What is justice?
Is it not our acknowledgment of rights,
an equitable distribution
among those acutely in need?

What is justice?
Is it not a willingness to listen,
an ability to act
with and on behalf of those closest to the issue?

What is justice?
Is it not a fusion of consciousness and conscience,
from which flows a capacity for critical reflection,
a context for the transformation of the world?

What is justice?
Is it not engaging the powers of the universe,
and discovering from this new capacity
strategic expressions to transform the world?

What is justice?
Is it not the manifestation of love
through acts of compassion
to heal the face of Earth?

What is justice?
Is it not spontaneous expressions of vision, possibility, hope,
the promise of freedom and pathways to peace
through wonder, solidarity and engagement?

Canticle for Geo-Justice

Where there are ruptures in creation
we are aroused to peace.

Where there is disquietude
we are invited to balance.

Where there is discord
we are attuned to resonance.

In and through the pain of our wounded planet
we are called to make our Easter with Earth.

From collapse and devastation
we discover within the risen heart of the universe:
cosmic peace,
profound harmony,
deep balance,
compassionate resonance,
Pentecost for our planet,
geo-justice with Earth.

In the early years of the ICCS program, the staff decided participants should have the option of choosing a focus for their study. The choices included sacred psychology, deep ecumenism and justice. On the evening following our staff meeting, a name came to me in my sleep: geo-justice. I brought it to the meeting the next day and it was accepted. Soon after, I composed this poem to give meaning to the focus on geo-justice in our program.

Geo-Wisdom

Life unfolds in gracious ways.
The doorbell rings.
A homeless one appears,
momentarily dispatched
with a meal ticket and
perhaps a place to sleep.

"Listen to the people,"
I hear an echo say.
Entrancing tales,
stories of deep oppression and fondest hope,
there are so many things to tell.

Reflect, describe and understand your life;
feel the urgency of now.
Pay attention to Earth.
She speaks of pain and peace and desolation,
while I am reminded of beauty all around,

Geo-justice calls out.
Mountains, rivers, birds and trees respond.
Feel the harmony, experience the balance,
let planetary peace survive.
Learn the story, tell the story
Let the story tell the story.
Let the story tell itself
through acts of compassion, creativity and depth.

Peek out from the precipice.
Each new moment becomes a prayer.
Welcome in a new adventure,
inaugurate another age.

Let your promptings be your guide.
Everything is sacred now,
a new chance for a mysterious alignment
between your actions
and the creative energy of the divine.

In the heart of the cosmos
and in the recesses of every soul
resides an unspoken hunger.

Embrace the wisdom of the universe
and all who dare to tell
of sacredness and depth.

May the scriptures of the heart,
pages of sacred texts
and the wisdom of the cosmos
converge in a fresh engagement
to heal our broken world.

Let each dawn and dusk
be a threshold to beauty,
wonder and
belonging all around.

With each new day
celebrate the gifts
of transformation and grace.

Discover fresh energy
to irrigate the soul of a planet,
as together we embrace
a future yet unknown.

Foreboding

There is a foreboding in the sky.
It hovers from on high,
about to pounce,
then vanishes and flies away.

War and rape and HIV
seem rampant in our midst.
They are the decline of Earth.

Listen to our planet,
hear her pain
announced by water and trees.

Heal us now, they cry,
send back the sun,
the flowers and the bees.

Bring joy to my heart.
Let wildness flourish
where promises are left.
May my foreboding disappear
and peace return to Earth.

Everything Is Wild

Aunt Margaret walks along,
bending occasionally for a berry,
but mostly enjoying the day,
breathing in the summer air
in the field where everything is wild.

Grab your honey pail,
head for the pasture behind the tracks.
Find wild strawberries in the open field,
flourishing in the sunlight.

Once Again

Walk softy in the meadow,
peer across the endless sky,
touch the soft green grass,
witness the golden sun disappearing in the West.

Experience every molecule of beauty,
each a sacred signature of God.
Let heaven happen now
as you await the sun once again rising in the East.

Monks of Skid Row

A strange breed of monks,
these 12,000 derelicts of life,
these lovable, genial, isolated human beings.
They live with a past not to be forgotten,
a present built out of isolation,
a future that promises and hopes
for nothing.

These monks of the inner city
are more alone than the strictest contemplative,
often more redeemed
as they traffic in their currency of cigarettes.
Where to get beer, a bed, a meal, a job
and sometimes money?
They are selfless and concerned,
these islands of humanity,
boasting of a day's work
and regretting a wasted life.

They trust NO ONE as they walk
their silent world of pain and fear,
this order of the street,
people without futures, without rights.
Poor, pushed, passed by and possessed
by those who provide beds and food,
keeping them on one aimless
treadmill of life.

It was summer 1970. I was a student at the Canadian
Urban Training Project for Christian Service in Toronto. The
director, Dr. Ed File, minister of the United Church of
Canada, had prepared us for what he called the "urban
plunge." We were to go into the ghettos with $5 in our

pockets and interact with the displaced persons we found there. The goal was to see people as they really are within a corporate system that necessitates winners and losers, rather than projecting stereotypes on them.

One evening, after going into the chapel for a bible service, I received a ticket and was assigned a bunk bed. As I sat on my perch on the upper bunk, I looked around the room and composed "Monks of Skid Row."

The Lamp Post

Leaning on that lamp post,
dizzy and uncertain,
he recedes and sinks
to the ground.

Intoxicated and almost unaware,
he sees his life go by,
as hopes and aspirations fade
even now.

Faint memories when times were good
momentarily return,
only to be washed away
by that deceptive bottle by his side.

Fractured

I wonder who that person is,
the one sitting on a plastic pail
in a shadow down on Shattuck.

I walk by,
then feel guilt,
a dollar still in my pocket,
an unpurchased paper still in her hand.
Did I deny her dignity?
Discomfort lingers in my soul.

The anonymous one
remains huddled in the shadow
wishes me, a passerby,
blessings of the day.

I wander home,
walk by Chez Panisse,
where the money people go.
A memory of the huddled one returns.

I arrive at home,
turn on the TV
hear the rich and famous
shouting from the stage,
asking for my vote.

Suddenly I wish the ballot box
could become a plastic pail.

Easter in Rehab

At the bedside of hope
I sit and wonder
about the mystery of it all.
Can illness bring hope?
Does apparent evil
always do us harm?

There is something in the soul
that answers the call of life,
comes to terms with terror,
transcends what seems hopeless
and arises to a new life.

Yes!
It's Easter in rehab.
Toxins give way to health,
fear is replaced by courage,
pain by healing,
companionship rather than
the illness of being left alone.

Yes! It's Easter in rehab,
where fragility and the toil of years
take on a noble glow.

The stone of despair rolls back
while we again discover
within the empty tomb of silence
a promise of new life.

Shadows

Shade shelters the maple
in the cool comfort
of a tranquil breeze.

Down across the meadow,
dance upon the shore,
experience the emergent power of
all that lies within.

Questions in the Rain on a Saturday Morning

Are not all our questions acts of faith,
and every uncertainty an urge and invitation
to what we desire and hold dear?
Is not all creation a banquet of beauty,
a generous gesture of friendship, intimacy and love?

Isn't the rain outside
a metaphor for tears that irrigate the land,
bringing springtime to my soul?

Today is another unexpected opportunity
to say thank you for my life
and give gratitude to God.
Each day is a challenge,
every new moment an opportunity
to realize that all I have received
is an unasked-for gift.

What is left to say and proclaim?
Perhaps gratitude is life's greatest gift.
Thank You.

Saturday in the City

Resonating beats
thumping through the streets
invade the contemplation
of urban dwellers today.

Midst troubled, violent sounds of death
people glide through perfumed halls
of conformity and cause.

Yet from interiority
may there still emerge
a simplicity that finds again
its source in every renewing indicator
of the heart.

Paying Attention

Paying attention is
the act of plunging
into the ocean of divine presence.

Paying attention is
the act of relocating divinity
within the depth of creation and self.

Paying attention evokes wonder,
and empowers us to do for others
that for which we pray.

To Look at Anything

I see the sun rising and moon in fast pursuit.
I feel something stirring.
Is it the mosquito on my arm?
Or the person in the chair beside me,
the one who seems distracted
by the crickets in the yard?

When I look at anything,
I realize everything is there,
memories of what I longed for,
recollections of the past not yet forgotten.

My days seem shorter now,
only an instant before the stars appear.
When I look at anything,
the universe is there,
a microcosm of all that is.

Listen

When someone deeply listens to me,
recognition happens.
Stories originate and flow,
loneliness dissolves.
The kitten on the back porch purrs
happily in the sun.
Spontaneity emerges.
Children break into song.

Listen, Listen!

When I pick up a pen to write a poem
the following happens.

I feel a stirring in my soul.
A revelatory moment rises and appears.
Memories flood my imagination.

Berries in the field, kittens on the porch,
Uncle Jerome's cigarette sending adoration to the sky.

Suddenly, I feel a mysterious, divine embrace.
The energy of love surrounds me.
What do I hear?
Listen, listen!

A whisper rising from the well spring of my soul,
till now unheard, softly calls from the depths.

Come here, listen,
I have much to say.

Perhaps about a less-traveled path
you are now called to tread.

Listen, listen!
Hear the silent voice
speaking from the cosmos on high.

I am invited be the poet and the politician,
called to make things happen in the world.

Listen, listen!
The ancient one now speaks.

Soft Echoes

When someone deeply listens to me,
I discover what is in the way.
I discover my way.

The fallen trees and broken sidewalk,
light in the darkness,
pathways through the forest.

Like a newborn
exploding into life and sound,
positioned to hear the dream.

The heartbeat
at first frantic then soft,
speaking of new life.

Molecule of Beauty

A soft haze floats in the fields this morning.
Blackbirds rustle in the trees.
Rabbits announce their presence
as they scamper
across the clover.

Meanwhile darkness floods the sky.
Stars and moon appear.
Then comes the rain,
the heavens empty torrents on us all.

Cattle gather under the great oak.
Together we endure the storm
and eagerly await the sunshine,
the return of peace,
while each drop of water
becomes a ray of beauty
across the land.

No Turning Back

There is beauty here,
here in this place,
the leaves turning red and gold.

The pastel sun shines
on a late afternoon.

Others with the gift of years
peer into the doorway of dusk.

Seasons change,
so do Earth and I,

wrapped in the irreversible
flow of life,

returning only to the source
of all that is.

In Between

Between the vision and the act
lies the shadow.

TS says so,
and I know it to be true.
So very true.

It is a lesson I have learned over and over again.

Change is not without struggle.
It seems always accompanied by turbulence.
Many have taught us this.

Yes, messiness is the place where life happens
in those in between times.

Origins

I came from the river,
cold winters,
ice on the pond,
cows in the pasture,
my father in his garden hoeing beans.

I came from French-Irish roots,
the hot spot in South Armaugh,
the French settlement by Lake Huron's shore.

I was a Catholic in a Protestant town,
where retired farmers lived and watched boats go by
from the front porches of their homes.

I came from Richard and Elizabeth's expanded heart,
raised in Sombra Village,
the land of ungiving clay.

I came from the fireball fourteen billion years ago,
which continues to flare forth today in supernovas,
exploding into I know not where.

St. Clair First Communion

A place where ferries sail, children swim,
fish jump and freighters sound their horns
as they sail across the channel,
the St. Clair River has been a poultice and my prayer.

It has united two countries,
been a metaphor of unity for a divided life.
It carried me and kept me afloat
when I feared I would be submerged.

It encouraged my struggle by its constant flow,
powered by Lake Huron above.
It showed me how to go forward
when I was about to falter.

When I was afraid to fall,
I was protected
from the toxins of psyche and soul
here on the shores of this great and joyous river.

I have walked upon these shores
both when I was happy and sad.
I felt the river's pain when the petrochemical industry
poured toxic sludge into its pristine water.

I crossed the border by ferryboat in summer,
I skated across it in winter.
When I felt the temptation to relent,
the river gave me encouragement.

When I lost my way, the enduring flow of the great St. Clair
was my friend, my focus and my guide.
Named after Clair, the lover of creation,
the great St. Clair sustained me and supported my journey.

The St. Clair River has been my spiritual companion,
my first communion,
my friend and guide.
May we flow together into our unknown future.

This Grace-Filled Morning

Recollections swim by,
times of peace and beauty.
Pickerel leap in the stately St. Clair.
Maple stands proudly in the yard.
Timmy the cat paws patiently on the screen door,
awaiting liberation.
Midst the blackberries and the corn
my father hoes patiently to watch his garden grow,
while robin in the backyard
wishes everybody well
on this grace-filled morning.

In Touch with the Sacred

Embrace the rose,
feel the sunshine,
tremble before the thunder and rain.

Gaze at the blackbird,
admire the great Canadian maple
standing in the yard.

Allow the sacred one
to touch your soul,
expand horizons beyond the farthest hill.

Intimacy abounds.

Modes of the Sacred

Feel magnificence.
Celebrate goodness.
Be moved by beauty.
Honor the radiance of life.

Broken Beauty

Memories flood forth
of the ninety-nine and one.

Terror and injustice roll across our land
like molten lava.

Sr. Simone stands tall before us, a voice for the voiceless,
the poor and underserved,

blocked from the ballot box
and the opportunity to celebrate and serve.

Meanwhile the electronic screen tells us tales
of things we do not need,

interspersed with campaign slogans detrimental
to our country and their cause.

Step back, breathe deeply
and take another look.

See the beauty in the streets.
Gaze at the world differently.

Become engaged.
As the song invited us long ago:
"Imagine a better tomorrow, give peace a chance."

Live Life, Not Write It

Engage the process,
feel the give and take,
venture an opinion,
dare to say yes or no.

In the midst of memory
forgive all that is past,
dive into every day,
greet the sunshine and the breeze,
sense the sun, snow and rain.

Now is the time to be alive.
Press the restart button.
Set aside the paper and the pen.
Welcome each day
as a new beginning.
Cast yourself on the waters of life.

Welcome to the Light

Sunrise dances in the far-off sky.
Windows in the heart and home greet new light.
There is now a new beginning.
Newness floods the world.
And once again with great anticipation,
we greet a new era and a new day.

Do Not Deny the Dream

As the networks drone on,
their familiar narrative of defeat,
with bated breath corporate storytellers
pronounce the outcome.
One more concession speech is heard.
Concessions in terms of
education
health care
Social Security
oppression of women
corporate control of government
the chasm between rich and poor
corporate greed and increased poverty
unemployment and under employment
ecological devastation and the illness of Earth
a misguided religion announcing "God is on our side!"
Yet deep in the heart of the people and the planet emerges
a transcending spirit that eclipses the concession into:
a heartbeat of hope for:
a people on the march
a vision of a fertile land
a dream not to be denied
a membrane that holds a new story
a context from within which beauty can shine forth
to illuminate a better tomorrow
with sunshine for the children,
with no concession, only hope!

Allurement and Letting Go

We have what we seek.
We don't have to chase after it.
It was there all the time.

The universe in all its magnificence,
friends new and old,
all good companions on the way.

Deep wells of insight
open themselves to our awareness
when leisure is our guide.

Earth speaks out of the silence
often in a hushed voice.

Listen, listen,
pay attention to what lies deep within.

You don't have to run after it.
It was there all the time.

Awake, rest and listen
to the recesses of your soul
and the vast wisdom that speaks
to you from the heart of the universe.

Our Self-Organizing World

Within the unrealized potential
of each of our lives
lies profound capacity to be who we are,
our destiny and purpose.

Caterpillar to butterfly,
acorn to oak tree—
in every creature,
fullness is contained.

Fulfillment
and self-realization
are the path laid out for us
at birth.

Properly supported,
encouraged,
our energy flares forth
into what we are called to be and do.

Plunging within ourselves
and out to the great universe,
we glimpse what we should do,
and go there.

These Days

Earth speaks.
Wonder, remember, listen.
Crickets in the pond have choir practice in the night.
Raindrops chant their slumber songs outside my window.
Foghorns echo from the river alerting all who stand below.
These days
I wonder, listen and remember
echoes from the back room of my soul.

The Gift of Clover

Clover in the field know their purpose,
to grow so green and sweet.
Bees come, spread their wings.

It's time to dream again, my friends,
to let our true nature flow.
Listen to the wisdom of the heart.

Discover there meaning for us all,
how to live and grow
and celebrate all we have been given.

Arc of Compassion

Wisdom flourishes and abounds.
Squirrel dances from limb to limb,
stops to look
then darts away.
Blackbird hovers in the sky,
surveying all of us below.

Puppies, birds and kittens
take their place in church
although already blessed
on this St. Francis Day.
All of life is gift, grace and promise.

Even asphalt jungle,
yes, the ghetto is a chapel
where homeless saints abide.
All is holy now,
nothing lies outside
the companionate embrace
of the wise and ancient one.

To Gaze Upon the Stars

Poetry and stories
tell of images and aspirations,
crafted in the seat of my imagination,
arisen from the floorboard of the soul.

Poems express luminosity,
encounters with mystery,
the road not yet taken,
adventures with lessons learned
at the crossroads of ecstasy and pain.

Now as I peer out my window on the world
I remember some of what remains unsaid
and strive to say it.

I gaze upon the stars,
feel deeply the urgency of now
to make a declaration to the world.

Immolation

Is there anything left to say
about mercy
about purpose
about life?

I think it's about shrinking
my false self,
dissolving illusion and blame.

And so I say,
may the pain of upset
and illusions
cleanse my heart.

May they bring back balance
that like dry embers
I am consumed by fire,
and in this immolation
discover peace and truth.

Prayers to an Unknown God

Turmoil surfaces.
Past pain
has another face.

Memories singe my soul.
Lacerations of the psyche
become an open wound.

Yet I hear another voice.
Yes we can!
Fired up!
Audacity of hope.
Fierce urgency of Now.
Ask not…
Nothing to fear.
I share a dream.
Blessed unrest.
Radical freedom.

Tomorrows transcend pain.
Peace deserves a chance.
Gratitude heals my greed and grief.

Tsunami of hope.
Peace.
Possibility.
Splendor.

Make our tomorrows better.
And trust in our known God.
Become a healing balm in Gilead
for our planetary soul.

Ordinary Prayer

What is more ordinary
than prayer?
Each moment
inaugurates a breath,
the inhalation
and exaltation
of existence.
Each moment
an invitation
to pay attention
to the wordless silence
of Earth.
Each moment
a choir of adoration,
a song of beauty.
The frog plays bass,
the cricket tenor,
together
a chorus of beauty,
a proclamation,
a cosmic melody...
an ordinary prayer.

SECTION II:

PAYING ATTENTION: PRAYERS

Prayer

Prayer once puzzled me, particularly the prayer of petition. "Is prayer a way to change God's mind?" I wondered. I prayed for my mother when she had cancer, but she didn't get well. Was my prayer answered? Did God say no? My catechism said that prayer was "the elevation of the heart and mind to God." What did that mean?

Later I began to understand that prayer was more about gratitude and praise than about "give me and forgive me." It was not about changing God's mind, but rather about changing my mind about God.

Today I believe prayer is largely about conscious self-awareness, about paying attention to the divine that is already present. In fact, prayer is more about listening and responding than about formulating words. It opens us to epiphany moments in every aspect of our life and throughout all creation.

Prayer happens in silence and solitude as well as in the events of our everyday lives.

Prayer enhances our awareness of "God's action in the world." Prayer can be understood as reading the news of the day; I recall that a friend told me he would read the newspaper each day "to see what God was up to."

Prayer is not a script, nor a resuscitation of prepared words. Through prayer we become consciously aware that our lives are enveloped in the divine presence. Our tradition advises us to "pray always," and in this way to remain aware that each day, moment by moment, we are bathed in God.

Prayer is embracing the dynamics of an evolving universe.

Prayer happens when we bring into consciousness the original flaring forth of the universe, the formation of the galaxies and planets, followed by the emergence of life and the human.

Prayer allows us to awaken to who we are and to live our story more fully each day.

Prayer infuses us with the energy needed to live with depth, hope, inspiration and purpose.

Prayer is an opportunity to acknowledge our membership in the community of creation, to live reflectively with Earth. It is more about being than doing, more about presence than petition, more about wonder and awe than redemption. Teilhard de Chardin counsels us to spend more time on creation and less on redemption.

Mary Oliver reminds us that prayer comes from noticing; it is an act of intimacy with all we encounter.

Meister Eckhart says, "If the only prayer you said in your whole life was 'thank you,' that would suffice."

He also asserts that if he spends enough time with a caterpillar, he will never have to prepare another sermon; in other words, every expression of creation is "soaked in God," permeated with divine presence.

Prayer is being with God in our journey through life. It means entering into the important moments in our life and the lives of others.

Prayer is embracing the dynamics of an evolving universe.

Prayer is living with spontaneity and compassion.

Prayer happens when we gaze at the beauty of the night sky or the bluebird caroling from a tree, as we search for language and symbols to express the inexpressible.

Prayer may be contemplating a sunset. It may be reflecting on the issues of life: birth, love, work, wonder and death.

Prayer is gratitude and acknowledgment.

Prayer is the deepest desire of our life, through which the divine is revealed in our midst.

Prayer is a conversation, a shared burden, a celebration of excitement.

Prayer means living in the soft embrace of divine energy that enfolds our presence and heals our pain. It is an opportunity to renew our deep-seated desire for a life of justice, peace, and renewed possibilities.

Prayer is paying attention to the breath of life, to the reality of doubt, to what could be.

Prayer is paradox. In unexpected moments when insight comes, stillness happens and we feel bathed in God. Prayer happens in turbulence and also in a quiet moment when we listen to an unfamiliar voice that offers guidance for the way ahead in the ever-present now.

Prayer is an encounter with mystery. It can happen everywhere and always; it is an approach and attitude, an awareness that "God is in all things and all things are in God."

Mystery Is God's Other Name

We attune our hearts to the rhythms of the universe;
we celebrate life and reflect on others whose lives are
themselves a prayer.
We become sensitive to the impulse of the spirit
as we remember the past, envision the future
and embrace the ever-present now.
Touched by numinous beauty, we participate in the
inhalation and exhalation of existence.
Today our call is to render thank yous for every gift to be
celebrated, recognized and seen.
Today we compose a litany for the soul as we send
proclamations of gratitude and praise—praise for our planet,
which finds expression in the cry of the wolf,
the heart of the bear and the mind of the mountain.
Now is the time to bring back our stories, recall our roots and
retrieve the gifts we have received and utter a collective
proclamation of "The Great Amen."
As we swim in a river of grace, we transform destruction and
take back our soul; ambiguity and risk become our guide.
We celebrate with great thanks that mystery is
God's other name.

New Modes

Emergence happens.
Life, ideas, good word
and incessant aspirations shine through.

Now it's time—today, this day, now—
for each of us and all of us together
to express what remains unsaid,
unheard, thought of or proposed.

Pray with your feet,
write what you have yet to understand,
tell tales and find your way back home.

May All People Be Free!

May justice roll like a river
flowing down to the sea,
dance, frolic and bounce
into the deep ocean of existence.
May beauty shine forth
for all that is.
Wonder and surprise
are my hope, promise and prayer.
May all people be holy,
all people be healthy,
all people be free.
Blessed be!

Blessed Are We

Blessed are we as cherished earthlings of God's wonderful creation.

Blessed are we whose humanity has been affirmed from the beginning of our evolutionary story.

Blessed are we who have been graced to embrace the unfolding paradox of creation in the unceasing process of birth-death-rebirth.

Blessed are we who, with creativity and an enormous capacity for innovation, are contributing to the building of God's Earth.

Blessed are we because we got it right for most of the time throughout our long history of seven million years.

Blessed are we who are forgiven by our large-hearted God for the times when we got things badly wrong.

Blessed are we as co-creators, committed to right relating in the name of love and justice.

Blessed are we because amid huge risk and misunderstanding, we dare to heal, forgive, liberate and empower those trapped in oppression, poverty and pain.

Blessed are we who have inherited open-ended parables, stories of inclusive liberation.

Blessed are we as custodians of the open table, symbol of creation's abundant resources, from which no one is ever to be excluded.

Blessed are we because Jesus bridges the way to our next evolutionary leap, illustrated in the empowerment of his resurrected presence.

A Litany of Transformation

Trust needs to be born,
security needs to die;
liberation needs to be born,
oppression needs to die;
celebration needs to be born,
boredom needs to die;
connectedness needs to be born,
alienation needs to die;
global awareness needs to be born,
nation-state-ism needs to die;
creativity and courage need to be born,
fear of death needs to die.

The right brain needs to be born,
the left brain needs to be happy about it;
feminism needs to be born,
patriarchy needs to die;
soul-making needs to be born,
individualism needs to die;
recovery needs to be born,
addiction needs to die;
playing together needs to be born,
competing needs to die;
the ecological age needs to be born,
environmental genocide needs to die;
reverence for all life needs to be born,
domination and objectification need to die;
doing-with needs to be born,
doing-for needs to die;
be-attitude needs to be born,
have-attitude needs to die.

Hope needs to be born,
despair needs to die;
creative silence needs to be born,
empty noise needs to die;
awareness needs to be born,
insensitivity needs to die;
circles need to be born,
hierarchies need to die;
dialectic needs to be born,
dualism needs to die;
laughter and tears need to be born,
sadness and sentimentality need to die;
a new order of geo-justice needs to be born,
the old order needs to die.

What Remains

When all passes
what remains?
When accomplishments and friendships pass
what remains?
When memories of every story ever told pass,
is it not the mystery of your presence that endures?
To this, to all that is and ever was, I say,
Thank you and Amen!

Plunge Me

Plunge me into depths of wonder,
to float among the stars.
Allow each supernova moment to be my guide.
Let the curtain that divides our lives depart.

Plunge me into nothingness, I cry,
let all questions rest.
Surrender to the great unknown,
where the sacred one abides.

Her Presence Itself Was a Prayer

Over the years I have been privileged to offer retreats and participate in Holy Week ceremonies at Springbank Retreat Center for EcoSpirituality and the Arts in rural South Carolina.

After one of these occasions, two sisters from the program graciously drove me to catch my plane at the airport in Myrtle Beach. I was in the back seat and Sr. Helen was driving. We admired the landscape, adorned with colorful flowers, which seemed particularly expressive of beauty on that Easter day.

Helen told me about the work she loved, visiting people in hospitals and prisons. As I heard her describe her work, I realized her presence itself was a prayer.

One Sunday, she said, she had arrived at a prison and was ushered into a holding cell. There she met a man named John, who was very distraught. His hair was tousled and his wrists badly scratched and bleeding. These were indicators of his attempts to do himself great harm.

The first words out of John's mouth were, "I'll speak with you, but as soon as you go, I'm going to finish the job."

Helen wasn't fazed. She took a seat and asked John to tell her about himself. She listened carefully, and when he spoke about his beautiful daughter, she suggested he might want to live to see her grow up to be a fine young woman.

When the guard knocked on the door and announced that visiting hours were over, Helen got up to leave. She looked at John and said, "I'll be here tomorrow. If you're dead, I'll pray for you. If you're alive, we'll talk."

John lifted his head and extended a hand to Sr. Helen. "I'll see you tomorrow."

Prayer from the Precipice

God of creation,
called forth by wisdom's crises,
we edge unknowingly
to the precipice of our era and time,
summoned by insight, intuition and You.

With grounded joy
we confront the options of our day
and collectively decide
to return and begin anew.

At this moment of hindsight and apprehension,
this time of depth and healing,
we are called to reinvent our culture and ourselves
here on the precipice of new beginnings.

Cosmic Presence

Begin your prayer of cosmic presence in a place of silence where you can gain a perspective on the world.

Recall the sacred moments of the great unfolding story, the original flaring forth, that moment when everything was born—the galactic time when through the explosion of light everything that exists today, every molecule and atom, came into existence and made possible the great geosphere that was to follow.

Reflect on the Earth and other planets coming into existence, and on Earth's balance of a molten center and outside crust giving birth to burgeoning new life. From the seas and waters, everywhere life began to stir, and grow and flourish upon the land.

From the depths of each psyche, and from the gratitude evoked by each expression of beauty, each new human awakens to the interconnected web of life that weaves the wondrous universe into a compassionate expression of belonging everywhere.

Through cosmic presence, we move from historical memories to this living moment of spontaneity, a lived experience of this sacred moment that floods our awareness with hope, and evokes and activates emergent energy all around.

Prayer for Engaged Cosmology

Let me be an instrument of engaged cosmology.

Where there is emotional turmoil, grant me clarity in my pain and foresight in my turbulence.

Where there are structures of oppression, grant me strategic approaches and the ability to act.

Where there is conviction that the dangers are too great or not at all, grant me critical reflection.

Where there is glum plodding and abstractions of tired forms of justice, grant me the fresh energy of geo-justice making.

Where there is the danger or irrelevance of only reaching out to the few, grant that I may be able to transform upset into moral outrage, systemic oppression into strategies for change, and cosmic consciousness into development of the work of engaged cosmology in a continuing journey of hope.

Engaged cosmology creates a synthesis of empowerment from a cosmic and cultural perspective.

Engaged cosmology views as one act the wonder of the night sky and the solidarity of people joined together in the work of empowerment and transformation.

Blessed be engaged cosmology.

Amen.

A Canticle of Hope

At this time, we are called to ignite a new meaning of hope. It is a time of expectation and perseverance.

A time of relationship and listening to the wisdom that resides in the recesses of our souls.

A time when through new moments of self-expression our imagination erupts and the divine becomes present in our lives.

A time to be aware of an emerging sacramentality being born in the minds and hearts of scientists throughout the world.

A time to reflect on a new cosmology that invites us to ponder the unfolding of the universe and humanity's place within it.

A time to appreciate nature as a promise rather than perfection.

A time to evoke positive energy; experience passion, pain and joy; and respond with integrity and unbridled potential.

A time of great expectations and yearnings for a future of promise and peace for the whole community of life.

A time to acknowledge the mystery of systemic change through an increased awareness that it is the divine that prays through us.

A time to respond to the desire for a global movement as we break down barriers and work for change.

A time to ponder the wisdom that comes to us from within a resacralized world that resonates with an inner sense of trust.

A time to foster a listening heart that rediscovers the divine presence in the poor of every species.

A time to embrace vulnerability, to be touched by the pain of the planet and the shimmering beauty of a bud about to flower.

87

A time to encourage the prophetic voice and support the formation of an ecological consciousness.

A time to embrace ambiguity and foster a dialectical awareness that will result in creativity and a hope-filled future.

A time to face our fears and take whatever risks are necessary to discover community and experience belonging.

A time to trust the depth of our deepest convictions, that they may move us out of the comfort zone of our existing community and into a new context yet to be formed.

A time to realize that "the future is in the living room," where people gather for theological reflection, dialogue, relationship, hope, information, energized action and support.

A time to embrace the messiness of these in between times as we strive to connect consciousness and conscience, process and action, in a free and fluid way.

A time to discover a cosmology that provides a context for personal, social and ecological change.

A time to ponder what the divine is inviting us to create.

A time to ingest the new universe story, with its mystery and emergence, calling us to a fuller and greater life that is functional and inclusive.

A time to engage in the shattering process of a paradigm shift that summons us to experience the death of the "Clockwork God."

A time to risk being on the margins of institutions and at the center of the issues that are critical for this moment.

A time to move beyond fear, to foster a new synthesis whereby we see a new cosmology that places us at the center of human suffering.

A time to discern and discuss through dialogue and silence where the new frontiers and challenges are in each of our lives.

A time for creativity that can heal the hole in our troubled hearts as we live through the dark night of our cultural soul.

A time to replace bullets with crayons and paintbrushes.

A time for creativity that fosters a wholesome sexuality that leads toward a mystical union with the divine and all that is.

A time to weave together the social and ecological gospels.

A time to celebrate and always be open to surprise.

A time to focus on an integration of mind and body, science and spirituality, and the cognitive and experiential.

A time to engage in the inward journey of personal change and the outward adventure of creativity and compassion.

A time to become empowered by a new literacy, a shared dream experience and a story that will reveal our role in the great work: the inauguration of a new era of well-being for the Earth community.

A time for a new global ethic that moves us away from a culture of consumption, competition and control.

A time to fashion a life-affirming planetary spirituality that is mystical, prophetic and transformative.

A time to celebrate a planetary spirituality that reveals our deeper destiny, embraces the new creation story, honors geo-justice making, is rooted in an expanded vision of our traditions and fosters intimacy and energy for the soul.

Mother of the Streets

I want to know how the child in you longs for home.

When you are frightened or alarmed by people of the streets, remember it is a dimension of yourself that walks there; that lives without address and documented identity and perhaps spent last night in a cardboard condo a park, a storefront or in the rain.

I want you to know your mother is with you on your journey. She accepts, embraces and loves you and welcomes you home to her heart. It is a welcoming heart, a heart of hospitality that feels the pain of unclean needles; the pain of exile and alienation; and the pain of rejection by self, other and the world.

I want you to know my heart is always open; my arms embrace you and my hands offer you bread for the journey, the bread of hospitality and nourishment of home.

I want you to know I am present with you in the streets, that you and your lifestyle are as dignified and worthy as those whose picket fences and gated communities keep out the public, the pain of the people and also me.

I want you to know this is a place of connectedness, that this is your home and the many relationships of the street are the monasteries of your life.

I want you to know that no matter where you are, wherever you sleep, however homeless you may feel, the street itself is a sacred place. It is a place for life, a place of nobility, a place of peace where good people and your Mother of the Streets also dwell.

I want you to heal your wound of homelessness, your wound of exile.

I invite you to come home to yourself, to your friends, even to your pain and of course, to the beautiful person you are.

I want you to come home to the street; home to your God and home to your Mother of the Streets, who welcomes you.

These words were composed in response to an invitation from China Galland, who for many years has conducted events on The Black Madonna and who led a weekend course at Sophia Center.

You Ask Me Why

This is why I'm here.

To listen with the ear of the heart,
to be an inclusive human presence,
open to the divine,
awake to the mystery of life.

I am here to respond
to what Earth is asking of me,
to honor the beauty of difference,
to celebrate the interconnected bond
holding us together and
honoring the soul of each member.

Proclamation of Trust

I believe in the gospel of life.

I believe it touches every aspect of our lives.

I believe the divine presence permeates every moment and place of our existence.

I believe all of life is sacred and sacramental.

I believe we are summoned by the gospel to a life of peace, prayer, compassion and justice-making.

I believe the call to work for the transformation of society and Earth is a special gift, an invitation to participate in building a community of empowerment on this fragile planet.

I believe what we most profoundly desire and know as just and true is rooted in tradition and the natural world.

I believe if we keep our hearts and minds open to the beauty and the crises of our time, we will make connections between our deepest convictions and what we are called to do.

Brothers of Earth

I have a dream
that I/we can be on intimate terms with all creation;
that I/we can move out from our isolation into
communion with all life;
that fear of life will be overcome by risk and trust;
that we can let go of our need to control, consume
and possess, by allowing ourselves to be in the here and now,
and by accepting what is given;
that we will learn to be intimate with ourselves so we
can be intimate with the cosmos.

I have a dream
that some day all the creatures of the Earth will live
with such trust and harmony that we can speak each others'
languages and dance together to the rhythm of the stars;
that there will be no more tears and terror, but
laughter and peace in all the communities of life;
that our rivers and oceans will sparkle like diamonds
in the warmth of our sun, and that life in these waters will
sing the hymn of the Earth;
that age will lead to wisdom, and wisdom beget
tenderness and compassion.

I have a dream
that the days of wantonly destroying the air, water,
soil and all the species and inhabitants on Earth will stop and
be replaced by a simple, generous balancing—taking only
what is needed for sustenance and sharing the surplus in
compassion with those who do without;
that the economic world and the living world will be
mutually supportive and harmonious.

I have a dream

of a garden, East of Eden, where men and women
work because there is meaningful work to do, not just to get
a paycheck;

in which children dig in the earth, sail on the seas,
wonder at the skies and play with the birds and animals in
the woods;

in which adults take time to care for the young,
nurture them and teach them the wisdom of Earth;

in which the old live out their lives in dignity and
wisdom as teachers, political leaders, guardians, storytellers,
travelers and wise investors of wealth;

in which human communities nestle into the
landscape;

in which the wild is still allowed to be.

I have a dream

that my grandchildren will be embraced by an
empowering educational system that nurtures their
individuality, supports their creativity, fosters their natural
tolerance and quickens their curiosity;

that every child will have the grace of playing in the
ocean, on the beach and in the grass;

that every adolescent will be gifted with profound
experiences of his or her Earth self and universe self;

that the demon of nuclear waste and fission will be
exorcised from the land;

that we can all walk in the sun, drink the water and
breathe the air without fear of diminishing our health;

that these experiences will be recognized as our
birthright;

that Earth will be seen not as an obstacle on the way
to soul, but as the way!

I have a dream

that human health care will be converted from a
system dedicated to crisis intervention and disease control to
a way of being informed by Earth-centered therapies,
mutually enhancing for the human and the other-than-human
alike;

that we will recognize in a practical and fundamental
way that Earth is our primary healer;

that through our encounter with ecotherapies that heal
our physical bodies, we will become aware of our ecological
bodies and heal our relationship with the rest of creation.

I have a dream

that the practice of peace will become prevalent in
the world;

that respect for diversity will blossom into
overwhelming and creative processes for healing differences
in the world;

that cultural differences will be celebrated and shared
throughout the land;

that we will learn from the lessons of the universe,
Earth and all the inhabitants of nature;

that continuous, lifelong learning and discovery will
become the norm throughout the world;

that the religions of the world will converge on a path
of spiritual awakening and common purpose;

that the resources of the world will be distributed
equitably to relieve unnecessary suffering and pain;

that young people will be invited into the center of
society so their ideas, curiosity and energy can be
incorporated and respected;

that all forms of intelligence and talent will be
recognized and respected as gifts of unique and equal value;

that individual and community needs will be
respected, met and celebrated.

Since 1997, a group of men have gather under the title Brothers of Earth to reflect on Thomas Berry's vision and explore its implications for their lives and work. On one occasion, inspired by his book *The Dream of the Earth,* we named our dreams for Earth and its peoples. This prayer is the result of our collective vision.

The Way Ahead

I want to live in a world—and contribute to its realization—that looks like this:

It will be a world where all of us awaken to our full potential and what is still possible to do.

It will be a world where science, art and oneness with the divine converge into a new realization of what it means to be human and alive to each new moment as it unfolds before us.

It will be a world where every tree, bird, fish and person realizes her fullest potential and contributes to the possibility of a better tomorrow.

It will be a world where programs and people gather with curiosity and courage to discover their original purpose and the fullest expression of who they are and why they are here.

It will be a time when each vast vision will coalesce into an overarching collective strategy, with tactics to make possible the fondest dream of each person who unites her energies and efforts to bring about the practical outcomes of this great awakening.

It will be a time when water is crystal clear, the air is like champagne and the sky azure blue.

It will be a time when we descend within our souls to a place deeper than analyses can measure.

Emergence and Surprise: A Midwife at the Floorboard of the Soul

Turbulence and joy become an emulsion of the soul when the wild imagination gives birth to each sacred impulse stirring in the heart of Earth, and in the fiber of each person crying out in urgent celebration for the meaning of life and the culminating gesture of resurrection and new life.

O great and creative One, we bring you our gifts, gifts that arise within the deep need to transcend and celebrate the beauty and brokenness of life.

We are here to resurrect; to live; and through engagement and surrender, to give birth, to bring into existence what was not here before and to honor the angst and surprise manifest in every flower, every butterfly and every life of nobility and purpose.

May tomorrow be a garden of celebration, an orchard of surprise, when all that we savor and celebrate shines through to give hope to many and aspirations to all.

May all of us give birth to divine nudges in the floorboard of the soul, give birth to new life and midwife a better world.

Companions on the Journey

Who accompanies us on the journey?
What is the process for the journey of the soul?
Are we not befriended by the stars?
Don't the sun and moon, daylight and dusk,
accompany us on our way?
There is so much to wonder about, so many hints that
accompany us.

It is the wise and noble one who is our companion,
who joins us as we rise and fall, and rise and fall again.
Deep in the heart of the cosmos and in the depths of
our soul, a beacon arises to guide us, a portal opens where
the ancient one invites us.

An open-ended invitation makes us dare to wonder,
to tremble and create a world where we decide to be present,
to look around and find within the pain and possibilities of
life the great unfolding of all that we cherish and hold dear.
Good companions on the journey are every star that
twinkles, every child that shivers with delight and every tree
and mountain that offer protection and show the way ahead.

We are not lost in the cosmos; the divine knows
where we are. Look up in the sky. Survey the road ahead.
Take the temperature of the times and challenges before you.
Join hands with all who wonder in the night, seeking
guidance, friendship and support.
You are not alone. The mountains and trees, sunshine
and stars, friends and companions know where you are.
Go forth, dear one, this way ahead is serious and
serene. Go forth, fulfill your purpose and you will find the
way.

Prayer for Going Forth

Divine source of love and life,
ancient one of ancient days,
empower us to be inclusive in all our acts
and an integral presence open to the indigenous peoples,
who perceive you in your many manifestations,
and always be aware of life's ultimate mystery,
palpable in the universe,
to empower us all to co-create
a more mutually enhancing world.

How Do You Pray?

It was a late December afternoon in Derry, New Hampshire, during the Christmas holiday. A friend of my brother asked a penetrating question: "What is your spiritual practice?" In other words, "How do you pray?"

Without much forethought, the answer came forth: "I walk, I read, I write."

I walk:

To walk is to take in the beauty of creation: to feel the gentle breeze, to survey the flowers and to greet the people and pets I meet.

It is during such walks that thoughts and feelings bubble up and come into consciousness. Perhaps questions hitherto left unasked now yield answers. For the most part, the walk is a time to read the book of nature and allow the images and sounds of the natural world to speak their wordless wisdom of beauty, touch and taste. And smell. Here, the God we do not know becomes present in the sights and sounds of each stride and moment.

I read:

When I read, I pick up books from theologians, cosmologists and spiritual writers who in their works and wisdom make significant connections between my lived experience and the eternal truths that are the legacy of my works and traditions. In these pages, the writings of Teilhard de Chardin, Thomas Merton and Thomas Berry are of particular significance. Others include Elizabeth Johnson, Rosemary Radford Reuther, Leonardo Boff, Judy Cannato, Diarmuid O'Murchu, Kathleen Deignan and many more.

However, in my reading I am also challenged to read the signs of the times and meditate on the hopes and dreams, challenges and transformative work of people who live at this time or in the past. Culture has its wisdom to tell and its challenges to present, as do our hearts.

I write:
When I write, I strive to make sense of my life, to create hopefully an integration between what I observe in my intra-psychic world and the world around me. I also seek to make shareable a dynamic integration of the cosmos and the soul.

SECTION III:

HABITS OF THE HEART: SPIRITUAL PRACTICE

Practice

Growing up in rural Southern Ontario, the family rosary was a practice insisted on by my father. It reminded me of who I was, although I often migrated to the softest chair on which to kneel. Now I look back on it with gratitude.

Other events in my early years indelibly imprinted on me the importance of spiritual practice. The Stations of the Cross was conducted weekly during Lent, led by the priest and myself as an altar boy. We recited prayers before each station numbered from Jesus' condemnation to death to his crucifixion and resurrection. There were also novenas, prayers to Mary, the mother of Jesus, for special assistance during challenging times in our lives. This was referred to as the Novena of Our Mother of Perpetual Help.

Other kinds of practices influenced me in my growing years. I watched ballplayers and boxers make the sign of the cross before going to bat or beginning a prizefight. My father planted potatoes on St. Patrick's Day each year, with the hope they would nourish us and compensate for the famine that had left our ancestors on the brink of death.

Spiritual practice can be understood as a response to these questions: How do you deepen and enhance your spiritual journey? What practices keep you in touch with the sacred dimensions, move you beyond what Alan Watts calls the "skin-encapsulated ego" and connect you to a wider vision of the world where you experience mystery amidst the ordinary?

For some, spiritual practice means spending time with the natural world—the ocean, mountains, rocks and trees. For others, it means consciously embracing the dawn and dusk of each day. Yet others may visit an art gallery, listen to music or read the words from a sacred text or a favorite author.

Spiritual practice can be a repetitive act, such as repeating the rosary or a mantra. The repetitive practice of reciting prayers can move our awareness to life's great mysteries.

In essence, spiritual practice is our way of discovering the movement of the spirit through a dialogue with everyday life. In our practice, we acknowledge what we love and become empowered to act accordingly.

Our tradition counsels us to pray always. To do so is to collapse all separateness between the sacred and the secular.

The wisdom teacher Sheng-yen advises us in our spiritual practice with these words: "Be soft in your practice.... Follow the stream, have faith in its course. It will go its own way meandering here, trickling there. It will find the grooves, the cracks, the crevices. Just follow it. Never let it out of your sight. It will take you."

Thomas Moore writes of spiritual practice with these words: "All we have to do is live this life with openness, imagination and a sense of paradox and wonder... Only by seeing through to the eternal and blissful soul of our neighbor will we catch a glimpse of the unnameable."

Thomas Merton, author, monk and scholar of the spiritual life, spent much of his life encouraging people to engage in spiritual practice or prayer; however, he never at any time told people how to pray. With this in mind, we can suggest that spiritual practice is how each of us discovers how to pray. The following are some of the ways people have engaged in the practice.

Find God in the Night Sky

When I was a student, I spent two summers at the Detroit Catholic Youth Organization as a camp counselor in Port Sanilac, Michigan, located on the shores of Lake Huron.

During each two-week session, we would take the boys on an overnight camping trip. As evening approached, we built a fire, roasted marshmallows and enjoyed the evening. Each time we had an overnight, the boys stayed up for hours and gazed into the stars. They were praying, even though they were not aware of it.

Even today as I remember these moments, I sometimes stand outside the chapel door at Holy Names University and look across the San Francisco Bay in depths of the night. In moments like these, something happens. I feel enveloped in a sense of mystery. Embraced by the divine presence, I am carried forward by a creative energy that courses through my life and that I can only name as God.

Heed the Prophets

Sometimes understood as Lectio Divina (reading a sacred text), this practice is rooted in an ancient practice. In times of anxiety, worry, preoccupation or need, good reading can be healing and energizing. I suggest you spend fifteen minutes a day with this practice.

The first act is to select a reading and listen to it. This can be from one of three types of scripture. One type is the universe story, made available to us through the wisdom of science. Another type is the scriptures of culture, whereby our experience of the divine is refracted through stories, customs, art and spiritual practice, as expressed through our experience of gender, ethnicity, race, class and region. The last type is the personal stories that linger in memory and can be told through movement, image, color and word. In each case, you simply listen to the reading and remain in silence.

The second act in the process is to hear the reading again. You reflect in silence once again. In silence you pay attention to the emotions that rise up in you as you let the words percolate in your psyche.

The third act in the process involves hearing the selection read a third time. Based on what you heard and understood the first time and what you felt and experienced in the second, you sink even more deeply into the experience. This time you become sensitive to what actions are prompted in you by the reading.

In this last phase, you may prefer to listen to soft instrumental music, which can support the earlier interludes of silence and enhance your experience.

You may wish to write down your responses and focus on whatever actions flow from the process.

Practice the Liturgy

As a cradle Catholic—and an ordained one at that—I value the practices of my tradition. Central to this is the liturgy. The word is understood as the work of the people, commonly understood as "the mass." There are two components.

The Liturgy of the Word: in this portion of the celebration, we read and listen to selections from the Hebrew Bible and New Testament. From these stories, we are nourished on our journey as we contemplate their relevance for our lives today.

The Liturgy of the Eucharist: in this portion of the celebration, we remember and make present the practice of Jesus, who gathered with his friends to celebrate the Passover meal that recalled the liberation from enslavement of the Hebrew people to freedom in the promised land. The Liturgy of the Eucharist is understood as the source and summit of the Christian life; through this great act of thanksgiving (the meaning of eucharist), we become empowered to care for the poor, sick, and our endangered planet.

Practice Hospitality

Fr. Reme Fumeleau, OMI, is a member of the Oblates of Mary Immaculate. He was born in France and immigrated to Canada soon after his ordination.

When he arrived in Yellow Knife in the Northwest Territories, Reme began an educational program in the Inuit community. His goal was to share with the Inuit people the basic tenets of the faith he had learned in the school of theology. Included in his curriculum were the Ten Commandments, the seven sacraments and other main components of his Catholic tradition.

When he had completed teaching the program, Reme wanted to conduct an evaluation to determine what his students had learned. He asked them, "Of all that I have shared with you about your faith, what do you consider most important?"

The immediate answer was: "Never lock your door!"

This came as a lesson for Reme.

He understood that, to the Inuit people, what was most important was not the static dogmas he had been teaching them, but rather the value of having hospitality in the cold climate of the far North. From the Intuit people, Reme learned that to be able to get out of the cold on a winter's night was a more powerful expression of faith than the ability to recite the creed or commandments of their tradition.

And so we practice hospitality. There are many ways to do this. You can welcome people into your home. You can invite them to share their interests and stories with you. Share a meal or recreational moment.

Food: Blessing and Artful Preparation

As a child, I was taught the following blessing before meals:

> Bless us, O Lord,
> and these Thy gifts,
> which we have received
> from Thy bounty
> through Christ, our Lord.
> Amen.

It is a blessing that endures even today. When I hear these words at a holiday gathering, I am reminded of the care my Aunt Margaret took as she brought to the table fresh, steaming hot loaves of bread. I also remember the food my mother cooked that echoed her cultural roots as a French Canadian—such delicacies as turtiar (pork pie), which she served us after midnight mass and on Sunday after church. My mouth waters now from these delicious memories.

Today, food has attained an expanded recognition for its place in our lives, as evident from Michael Pollan's writing: originally *The Omnivore's Dilemma: A Natural History of Four Meals,* and most recently, *Cooked: A Natural History of Transformation.* Also, First Lady Michelle Obama has launched Let's Move, a national campaign against childhood obesity that aims, among other goals, to teach habits of healthy eating.

Food is truly a precious gift. We feel this strongly when we recognize that we must eat to live, yet know countless children around the world are dying of hunger in this very moment.

To bless your food is a spiritual practice of gratitude and creativity.

You can participate in blessing your food in many ways. While cooking, you may choose to listen to sacred music. When you sit down for a meal, offer a blessing before you eat. You may wish to use the prayer I included here or one from your own family tradition. I also invite you to create your own blessing, much as the prayers included in this book were created.

Claim Your Roots

Gino Baroni was from Allentown, Pennsylvania, and he used to talk about his Italian childhood and the importance of his ethnic roots and identity. As a boy, he would go into the basement of his family home to help his father make wine. He borrowed his mother's white galoshes and climbed into the large vat of grapes and jumped up and down on the grapes to start the winemaking.

As he grew older, Gino was saddened by the melting pot metaphor, whereby people lost their ethnic identity and became amorphous Americans. He used to say with great passion, "The trouble with white Americans is they are like Wonder Bread—they have no color, and they have no crust. They have no story."

Gino was in favor of a vertical mosaic, whereby each person could claim and celebrate his or her ethnic identity and roots, and his or her dreams.

Fueled by this belief, he founded a program called The National Office for Urban Ethnic Affairs. He also was appointed to the position of assistant secretary for the Office of Housing and Urban Affairs. When Jimmy Carter was president of the United States, Gino was on the board of the Catholic Committee on Urban Ministry, which was how I got to know him.

Inspired by Gino's story, claim your own cultural identity and roots. Know the foods and diet of your heritage, as well as its music, art and literature.

As you claim your roots, respect and invite your friends and colleagues to do the same.

Practice Compassion

When we practice compassion, we acknowledge the divine that surrounds us. We are able to expand and at the same time feel secure, conscious of the words of Meister Eckhart: "The best name for God is compassion."

When we practice compassion, we embrace equality with all whom we are called to serve, be it the person, the river or the tree.

Compassion is related to pain, even cosmic pain. In other words, when we extend our awareness of our pain to the pain of Earth, we move into compassion. Rabbi Heschel said, "God suffers when man suffers." Compassion is, in a very real way, about relieving the pain of God.

Compassion is about healing.

Not everybody participates in protest marches, not everybody goes to the soup kitchen, not everybody goes to an AIDS hospice, not everybody saves the whales. We are called to our unique dimension of compassion. Justice-making needs to reflect our diversity. Some people need to go to the library, other people need to go to the streets and yet others need to go to the garden.

Compassion is about a new heart, a new structure and a new consciousness flowing out of the art of our lives. We connect with each other, with ourselves, with Earth; that's geo-justice.

Compassion is not elitist. It is not about pity or feeling sorry for others. Its tradition is born out of a shared interdependence and a sense of awe. We live in the fetal waters of cosmic grace. Not only must we celebrate this, but we must struggle for those in our midst who are deeply wounded by poverty of soul or body.

Each of us is aroused to a different act of justice-making. Each of us sees the *anawim* (the biblical word for the poor and voiceless) in a different guise. The planet is the

114

anawim of today, and so are women, racial minorities, animals, rain forests and many others.

Be aware of the issues of the poor of the world and your community. Cultivate a lifestyle that promotes justice and peace.

Practice an all-inclusive spirituality whereby all your relationships are predicated on reciprocity and empowerment.

Energize Relationships

Years ago, on the streets of Toronto and Chicago, I learned a lesson that has been with me ever since: Listening and recognition are two important gifts we can extend to others.

When we listen and recognize another person, many stories can emerge.

As humans, we have the gift of self-reflective consciousness. We are at the root of our lives storytellers. This is how we communicate and how we name our identity as a family, neighborhood, country and as people of the cosmos itself.

By listening and recognizing others, we energize our relationships and weave together webs of relationship that reveal who we are and that empower us to act.

The Pacific Institute for Community Organization (PICO) program begins its training with what they call "one-on-ones." This is a session in which two people engage in a conversation. They get acquainted, learn about each other's interests and concerns, and discover what people would love to accomplish in their neighborhood to improve their lives.

Whenever you speak to another, listen carefully to what he or she has to say. Offer your recognition and respect through your active listening. To engage fully in the art of conversation in this manner is in fact a form of prayer and a spiritual practice.

Relate to the Little Ones

When we relate to children, we follow the example of great prophets and mystics. Meister Eckhart said, "If I were alone in a desert and feeling afraid, I would like a child with me."

To connect with the divine, allow yourself to be close to a child, based on the conviction that God is more present in the little ones.

Time spent with a child—perhaps the son or daughter of a friend—is time well spent. Programs such as Big Brothers Big Sisters create the opportunity for companionship with a young person, and provide a source of guidance perhaps lacking in the young person's life.

As those youngsters mature, many later feel deep gratitude for the man or woman whose friendship and support inspired them to accomplish great things at a time when no other caring adults were present in their lives.

Spend time, as well, with other little ones—such as young animals or flowers about to bloom. These will provide the energy and spontaneity of youth to comfort and engage the soul.

Never Negate the Light

It was a cold, rainy night in November, clouds hovering heavy in the sky, blocking the crescent moon. Hardly a car was on the road as a late model Honda sped through the countryside.

Unexpectedly its motor began to sputter, and soon the car came to a full stop.

The man at the wheel peered at the dashboard, his eye fixing on the needle, now resting far to the left. He'd run out of gas!

For what seemed like an endless moment, the man sat motionless. Then he noticed what appeared to be the light from a distant farmhouse.

Rummaging in the trunk, he found a tattered umbrella that would at least partially protect him from the soft but relentless rain. Then he made his way along the road toward the light glimmering in the dark. The last thing he wanted was to be imprisoned in a car out of gas on a cold, rainy night.

As he drew near the farmhouse, expectations about the response he might receive began to circulate in the man's imagination. Would he be welcomed and offered the opportunity to dry off, be given a cup of hot tea and gas for the car?

He reached the gate and climbed the steps to the front door. Just as he was about to knock, an unexpected assertion sprang to mind: "Keep your gas!"

With those involuntary words ringing in his head, he beat a hasty retreat from the house and retraced his steps to the fuel-less car, where he spent a long night awaiting assistance from the first willing passerby.

How easy it is for our habits of mind to undermine our fondest wishes and goals.

One negative thought can cancel out so many possibilities, so much potential. Rather than anticipate self-imposed disappointment, it is so much better to focus on that proverbial light in the window that can serve as a harbinger of promise that our hopes will indeed be fulfilled.

And so we practice a positive outlook.

We welcome the generosity and good will of others when we are in need, rather than cut ourselves off by anticipating a negative response. We vow never to negate the light in the dark that draws us forward.

Let Go

I have often said the primary act of the spiritual journey is letting go. Meister Eckhart who wrote, "Unless you let go, you cannot reenter" and "God does not ask anything else of you except that you let yourself go and let God be God in you."

Through the practice of letting go, we become liberated and free. Whether we are Sufi, Christian or Jew, we let go and realize at a deep level we are not in charge of the universe, including our own world.

To trust the unfolding dynamics of the universe is to allow the mental categories of control to diminish. Dom Helder Camara, former Bishop of the Poor in Recife, Brazil, said it this way: "Accept surprises that upset your plans, shatter your dreams, give a completely different turn to your day, or even to your life."

Letting go is the number one spiritual strategy in response to the bitter and burdensome aspects of existence.

We let go of any way that we have neglected to forgive others who may have offended us.

To let go is to become deeply convinced that we are healable, that we were born into a world of original goodness. When we let go of the conviction that we are unhealable, we allow ourselves not only to heal others but to heal ourselves.

Remember to Grow Your Soul

One summer day after my former high school baseball coach, Roy Tennyson, died, I went to visit his widow, Dorothy. When I arrived at her house out in the country, she was taking a walk in her backyard orchard.

As I approached, I greeted her and asked how she was.

Her response has stayed with me over these many years: "I'm just out here in the backyard growing my soul," she said.

Perhaps what Dorothy meant that day on the farm was "I am remembering. I'm making sense of my life. I'm missing my husband Roy of many years. I'm learning the lessons of life from the trees in the orchard and from the companionship of my dog. I'm seeing all of life and the beauty of creation as a theater in which to learn and celebrate."

When I and all of us are asked what we are doing in our dwelling place, may we, like Dorothy, respond, "I'm just out growing my soul."

Remembering connects us to the experience of love and the vitality of the soul.

In remembering we connect to family, tradition, universe, ancestral roots and the society in which we live. When we remember we speak from the center of our sacredness and are prompted to tell the truth and reveal divine communication moment by moment in our lives.

Be Receptive to Beauty

Two friends were on vacation visiting the Grand Canyon. One had normal sight, the other was blind.

As they stood by the guard rail overlooking the canyon, the person with normal sight was looking around, distracted by the tourists and an airplane soaring above.

Meanwhile the blind person "peered" into the canyon, and while doing so, tapped his friend on the shoulder. "Isn't it beautiful," he exclaimed, "isn't it beautiful?"

Instantly, the sighted man was startled into a new awareness of his surroundings. Clearly, his companion could not see the vast beauty of the Grand Canyon; however, he was able to imagine the beauty before them with the eyes of his heart.

When we experience nature through any one of our senses, we experience the divine.

We can learn more from the trees and the stones than we can from the books of the masters. It is the beauty of creation that will heal the hole in our hearts and make wonder, beauty and belonging possible.

St. Benedict, founder of monastic life, advised us to "listen with the ear of the heart." With this in mind, we remain open and receptive to the voices of the bird, the tree, the kitten and the pond. All speak the language of creation and are expressions of the divine voice that communicates in so many ways.

Become aware that the God of the cosmos is present in every blade of grass. When we are touched by ultimate mystery, our lives are transformed and we move forward to take an inventory of our gifts, become wrapped in mystery and engage in the great work.

Shared Dream Experience

To remember and reflect on our dreams is a spiritual practice. Dreams can be thought of as the language of the divine; Carl Jung wrote, "The dream is the divine voice and messenger."

Dreams can be understood as revelatory insights into what lies deep within.

One spiritual practice is to write down your dreams and visions and share them with others in conversation and on paper. I have a notebook on my night table so I can capture any fragments of a dream that remain available when I awake.

I recall asking Thomas Berry about the operative principles for putting his work into practice. His answer has stayed with me, "It's all about story and shared dream experience." Thomas was not referring simply to the personal symbols that are revealed to us in our nightly dreams; dreams also can be understood as archetypal. In that sense, even a fragment of a dream can provide wisdom and insight for the totality of our lives and show us how we can move forward into the future.

The word dream appears in the title of Thomas's award-winning book, *The Dream of the Earth*. He is speaking about a vision that becomes available to us from beyond conscious thought, a vision that can energize and empower us for the work that lies ahead. His own vision was of a more mutually enhancing world that he termed the ecozoic era, in which e our lives would be guided by reciprocity. This was his dream for Earth.

We build community and celebrate friendship when we are able to say to each other, as we offer insight and compassion, "If this were my dream…"

This is a spiritual practice that will widen our horizons and expand our capacity to make the world better.

Empowerment Practice

This practice can be accomplished alone or in a group.

1. Select an issue in which you are interested.

2. Complete the following tasks. If you are in a group, divide into three smaller groups so each can do a different task.

- Compose a letter to an important decision maker or world leader in which you address the issue you selected.
- Create an artistic response to the issue; it could be through movement, music, image, song or another creative form.
- Decide on a strategic action through which you can confront or resolve the issue. If you are in a group, focus on a collective action. Describe how this action can be accomplished.

3. For closing, compose a poem, prayer or practice that addresses the issue and creatively places it in a sacred context. If you started in a group, come back together and do this as one group.

Silence the Mind

You can never have enough opportunities for silence. In today's dysfunctional culture of 24-hour news cycles; Musak in elevators, stores and restaurants; and iPods and cell phones in constant use, we are distracted and diverted to superficial concerns. We need silence in our lives. More than the mere absence of sound, we need a silence that provides relief from what Thomas Merton calls "an inordinate self-consciousness," a silence that allows thought to come and go, neither resisted nor clung to.

Silence can connect you to the well spring of your life, enrich your journey and foster the possibility of an inward space from which intuition and self-knowledge emerge.

An important question for each of us on our spiritual journey is "Is there enough silence in my life?"

Silencing the mind can be practiced in the following way.

Find a place where you will not be disturbed. This could be a room in your home or a sanctuary you find for yourself.

Sit comfortably with your legs uncrossed and feet firmly on the ground or floor. Pay attention to your breath, with normal intervals of inhalation and exhalation.

As thoughts come to you, imagine them as fish swimming by in a bowl: they appear, stop for a moment and continue on. You neither resist nor follow them.

Over a period of minutes, you can create a distance from whatever is happening in the external world, as well as from the internal chatter. In this way, you are able to quiet the mind.

You may experience the voice of the divine speaking to you and grounding you in the depths of your being.

Honor the Dawn and Dusk: Moments of Sacred Presence

The mystical moments of dawn and dusk are sacred thresholds when the universe, a manifestation of the divine, reveals itself. In these special moments of intimacy, the veil between the worlds of day and night lifts and we become conscious that we live within these two dynamic gestures of divine presence.

Through the practice of pausing to honor dawn and dusk, we become pilgrims of a new mysticism. We honor the luminal moments with great gratitude for the mystery of existence. In profound silence, we engage and celebrate these sacred moments.

Celebrate the Solstice: Light Arrives and Disappears

Since ancient times, all cultures have celebrated the solstice. At these junctures, we experience the major shift that occurs in the relationship between the sun and Earth.

On December 21, we mark our darkest day, when the sun begins to return. In the Christian tradition, this event is met with the celebration of Christmas, when believers mark the time that the Son of God became present to Earth dwellers in human form through the birth of Jesus of Nazareth.

The summer solstice on June 21 marks the longest day of the year, when we experience the most light. Here, we recognize that from each day forward we will experience shorter days and less light, until the winter sun again begins the long journey back toward summer.

These solstices are times when, steeped in a profound awareness of the sun's generosity, we gather to honor this sacred source. We extend our awareness to the movement of the planets and pay homage to our planetary spirituality by gratefully celebrating the centrality of the sun and its meaning in our lives.

Solstice is a time for personal change and cultural transformation. It is a time to cleanse, purify and protect. It is a time to name our hopes for a new era, to become midwives for peace and balance and to envision a better tomorrow through movement, chants, silence and songs.

At each solstice moment, we pray that a new day will be born—not the end of the world, but the end of this world as we know it, filled with ecological devastation, the destruction of beauty and the desecration of life.

In the dark of the longest night, may something new be born: a new era that will illuminate our hearts and shine in the world, with promise for a magical moment that will heal, renew and regenerate the time about to be born.

In a similar way, the summer solstice brings promise of harvest, fruitfulness and good and bountiful days ahead.

May we gather as companions on the journey to dissolve all fear, and with joyful anticipation await the new days that lie ahead.

Create Congruence: See, Judge and Act

Inspired by the writings of Leonardo Boff, which address the development of the church through base communities, people have gathered to follow a threefold practice: see, judge, act. This approach, sometimes understood as Catholic action, has its roots in the writings of Cardinal Joseph Cardijn of Belgium and can be dated back to the nineteenth century work of Leon Olle-Laprune.

The practice can be conducted alone or in a group. The result can be understood as naming our operative theology, which is understood as that dimension of our spiritual tradition that prompts us to act and create congruence between our vision and values and how we act in the world. The three moments of the process are understood in the following way:

Moment I: See

In this first moment, you are invited to view with compassion and mercy the impact of our world, whether it be social, cultural, political or planetary. Look around and take an inventory of the issues and concerns that affect your life. This might involve focusing on the economic disparity between the rich and poor, or on your concerns about work, family, ecology or social injustice.

Moment II: Judge

At this stage of the process, look around and examine how your spiritual instinct or values either affirm or critique the issues identified in Moment I. The practice can include reading a passage from scripture that addresses the issue. For example, if your focus is on poverty and the treatment of the economically disadvantaged, the passage could be The Sermon on the Mount and "Blessed are the poor."

Moment III: Act

Here the process involves discerning a personal and/or collective action that is responsive to the issue identified in Moment I and empowered by the reading reflected in Moment II.

Again, if the issue is poverty, an appropriate and timely action could be to participate in a soup kitchen to feed the poor or bring used clothing or canned goods to a St. Vincent DePaul or Salvation Army facility.

EPILOGUE:

GRATITUDE FOR ALL THAT PREPARED US FOR THIS MOMENT

The journey of the sacred butterfly continues from larva to chrysalis and ultimately to butterfly as our lives unfold.

As people of poetry, prayer and practice, we express gratitude for all that we have received from parents, tradition and culture. We imagine a world that transcends static dogma and imposed patterns of living. We feel moved by life's ultimate mystery and gaze realistically at this critical time in human/Earth history.

We approach each new poem, prayer and practice empowered by a vision of the world as we would like it to be in a future that is ours to create, a world where it is possible for beauty to shine forth.

Energized by the prophetic voices of yesterday and today, we gaze with wonder at the vast universe before us and in contemplative moments listen deeply to the scripture imprinted in our hearts.

The world offers so much beauty: a puppy exhilarated on his evening walk, the greeting of a loved one after a time away, visiting a friend in the hospital to receive word of his remarkable recovery from a mild stroke, a sunset over the Pacific that takes our breath away.

These holy moments, when the heart is full and hunger quenched, happen every day. Even in the face of illness and uncertainty, beauty and gratitude remain. Rivulets of gratitude flow from the sacredness of what previously appeared to be an often-broken heart.

At these and countless other times, we express a breath of gratitude to the ancient one of ancient days, who sustains and guides us on these untrodden paths. To thank and praise these moments is an act of prayer, an acknowledgment of the divine creative energy guiding and celebrating our lives.

Give Thanks

Every morning announces newness.
Every dawn an opportunity,
a gratitude moment.

Every new day
a reminder.

Give thanks.
Praise the world.

Be at peace.
Live well.
Bless each tomorrow.

ALSO by Jim Conlon:

Beauty, Wonder and Belonging*: A Book of Hours for the Monastery of the Cosmos* invites the reader to engage the rhythms of the day to explore the mystery of the divine and the human experience unfolding within the Universe. Stepping over the threshold of each dawn and dusk, our origin story reveals our sacred purpose within the Great Work.
ISBN: 978-155605-3995

Invisible Excursions: A Compass for the Journey, Jim Conlon discusses the evolution of culture and theology over the past decades, which he has organized into a series of seven epochs. Simultaneously, he traces what he terms "invisible excursions"—that is, experiences that touch all of us at a deep level, and that over time allow new understandings to germinate within us and lead us into uncharted territory. *Invisible Excursions* is part memoir and part cosmological commentary.
ISBN : 978-155605-4433